BOTTLENOSE
DOLPHINS

Paul Thompson & Ben Wilson

Colin Baxter Photography, Grantown-on-Spey, Scotland

BOTTLENOSE
DOLPHINS

First published in Great Britain in 1994 by
Colin Baxter Photography Ltd
Grantown-on-Spey
PH26 3NA
Scotland
www.worldlifelibrary.co.uk

Reprinted in 1996
New edition 2001

WorldLife Library Series

A CIP Catalogue record for this book is available from the British Library.

ISBN 1-84107-116-1

Photography Copyright 1994 by

Front Cover © Flip Nicklin (Minden Pictures)
Back Cover © Doug Perrine (Innerspace Visions)
Page 1 © Ben Wilson
Page 4 © Doug Perrine (Innerspace Visions)
Page 6 © Francois Gohier (Ardea)
Page 8 © Pete Atkinson (Planet Earth)
Page 9 © Ben Wilson
Page 10 © Doug Perrine (Planet Earth)
Page 11 © Doug Perrine (Innerspace Visions)
Page 12 © Flip Nicklin (Minden Pictures)
Page 15 © Ben Wilson
Page 16 © Doug Perrine (Innerspace Visions)
Page 19 © Flip Nicklin (Minden Pictures)
Page 20 © Sarah Curran
Page 23 © Doug Perrine (Innerspace Visions)
Page 24 © Paul Thompson
Page 25 © Francois Gohier (Ardea)
Page 26 © Doug Perrine (Innerspace Visions)
Page 28 © Ben Wilson
Page 29 © Ben Wilson
Page 31 © Flip Nicklin (Minden Pictures)
Page 32 © Doug Perrine (Innerspace Visions)
Page 35 © Top Thomas Henningsen (Marine Mammal Images)
Page 35 © Bottom Paul Thompson
Page 37 © Silvan Wick (Marine Mammal Images)
Page 38 © Ben Wilson

Page 39 © Top Left Ben Wilson
Page 39 © Top Right Laurie Campbell
Page 39 © Bottom Left Ben Wilson
Page 39 © Bottom Right Ben Wilson
Page 40 © Flip Nicklin (Minden Pictures)
Page 43 © Ben Wilson
Page 44 © Doug Perrine (Innerspace Visions)
Page 46 © Kevin Schafer (NHPA)
Page 47 © Ben Wilson
Page 49 © Top Sarah Curran
Page 49 © Bottom Doug Perrine (Planet Earth)
Page 50 © Flip Nicklin (Minden Pictures)
Page 52 © Ben Wilson
Page 54 © Laurie Campbell
Page 55 © Ben Wilson
Page 56 © Doug Perrine (Innerspace Visions)
Page 58 © Randall Wells (Marine Mammal Images)
Page 59 © Flip Nicklin (Minden Pictures)
Page 60 © Paul Thompson
Page 63 © Ben Wilson
Page 64 © Ben Wilson
Page 65 © Henry Ausloos (NHPA)
Page 66 © Flip Nicklin (Minden Pictures)
Page 69 © Doug Perrine (Planet Earth)
Page 70 © Paul Ratcliffe (Marine Mammal Images)

Printed in China

Contents

Introduction

As the morning sun strengthens, its rays catch the blue of an oil rig supply ship ploughing its way west through a calm sea. While the rest of the crew sleep, the second mate and radio engineer pace up and down the bridge to stay alert. With a yawn, the engineer leaves and wanders down to the front of the ship. Smoking, he looks idly over the bows to see the ship cutting through the glassy water.

For a minute or two he watches, letting his eyes drift in and out of focus as the dark silky water rushes past. Then, all at once, the sea below him is filled with shapes and energy as bottlenose dolphins rush in from either side of the ship. Three from one side and two from the other. Below the astonished onlooker, the five olive-colored 'torpedoes' join and huddle together. Racing just ahead of the unremitting mass of steel, the dolphins twist and turn, crossing each other's paths just inches below the surface. Effortlessly they move in front of the ship as if held in an invisible force field, their dorsal fins vibrating as the water rushes past them. One starts to roll over and over, as another emits a stream of bubbles from its blow-hole. Others do the same, and then, suddenly, they scatter.

In a moment they regroup and the outermost dolphin peels off to the side. Rising to the surface he shatters the glassy water with a 'puuwwf', exhaling and inhaling almost simultaneously. Gliding below the broken water he flicks his tail powerfully and rejoins the pack.

As the others leave to do the same, one animal turns to look up at the ship and the man craning over to see them. For a moment the two species hold eye-contact. Then, as suddenly as it appeared, the group re-forms and vanishes to the east. The engineer shakes himself out of the spell and lifts his shoulders away from the barrier. In a daze he wanders back to the bridge, pondering a lasting memory of the dolphins' physical grace and inquisitive nature.

Over the years, both mariners and landlubbers have enjoyed these brief moments in the company of dolphins. But of all the forty or so species to be found in the world, it is the bottlenose dolphin which has become our stereotype. If we have not encountered bottlenose dolphins in a dolphinarium, the chances are that we have seen them on television. For those of us not witness to repeat after repeat of 'Flipper' TV shows, bottlenose dolphins can now been seen smiling at us from advertisements for everything from washing powder to new windows.

With exposure to these animals we have also seen increasing demand for the protection of whales and dolphins and their marine habitats. Much of the scientific research carried out on these species has been stimulated by these demands. But few of us lucky to be involved in such work can deny that we are driven also by something deeper. The dolphins' marine world is quite alien to us and we remain fascinated by how they have adapted to this environment, and how the constraints of their surroundings shape their lifestyle.

Boats often attract dolphins.

Slowly, through the efforts of amateurs and professionals throughout the world, we are coming to understand more, but there is still much to learn. We hope that this book serves to stimulate both an appreciation for bottlenose dolphins and a desire to understand more about them and their underwater world.

Bottlenose dolphins are one of the most widespread and best known
of marine mammals. Their underwater world remains alien to most of us,
but an increasing awareness of these animals has led to demands for
the protection of both the dolphins and their marine habitats.

Mammals in the Sea

The bottlenose dolphin belongs to a group of marine mammals which includes whales, dolphins and porpoises. Collectively, they are known as cetaceans (from Latin *cetus*, Greek *kétos*, meaning whale). The cetaceans are not particularly closely related to other marine mammals such as seals and manatees. Nevertheless, like other mammals, marine mammals all have warm blood, depend upon air to breathe, and produce live young which feed on milk. What makes cetaceans unusual as mammals is that they have adapted to a life where they can reproduce and feed in the sea.

In recent years there have been some fanciful claims that humans are close relatives of dolphins. Features such as our large brains and lack of fur have been used as evidence to support this. However, while our nearest relatives are the apes and monkeys, cetaceans are more closely related to ungulates, hoofed mammals such as pigs, deer and hippopotami. In many ways, it may be easier to think of similarities between ourselves and dolphins than, say, a llama and a dolphin! However, from the study of the anatomy of living animals and the bone structures of fossils, it seems that cetaceans and ungulates have a common land-based ancestor: a small shrew-like animal which lived over one hundred million years ago.

This creature's descendants evolved to produce the ancestors of the modern ungulates and a group of ancient whales known as the Archaeocetes. These animals began to spend more and more time around and within lakes, rivers and seas. Gradually they evolved into many different forms which were better adapted to permanent life at sea. Their body forms changed to suit the watery medium and the four-legged animals took on a more streamlined appearance. In the history of the cetaceans, like a multi-million-year-old soap opera, hundreds of species and families came and went, many body shapes appeared and vanished. Only a few survived. One group which failed was the unlikely sounding Squalodontiids. Appearing around thirty million years ago, they were rather like modern river dolphins, but with up to a hundred tiny shark-like teeth. Within five million years they were gone, leaving no representatives for us to see today.

We are witnesses to the latest episodes in this ongoing saga. Although we may not be watching the heyday of the whales, we can still see a fascinating diversity of species, many of which seem almost as strange as their prehistoric ancestors.

Although we often refer to this wide group of species as whales, dolphins and porpoises, these three groupings misleadingly split the animals up by size rather than by any evolutionary order. For example, the killer whale is large and therefore called a whale, but it is more closely related to the bottlenose dolphin than to many whales, and would be more appropriately called a killer dolphin! In addition, the names given to species often vary from place to place. The bottlenose dolphin has been known as the gray dolphin, black dolphin and bottlenose porpoise. Even where people agree on a name they seem to differ in their spellings, resulting in bottlenose, bottlenosed and bottle-nosed dolphins. To overcome this confusion, each species and sub-species of animal and plant also has a scientific name. The bottlenose dolphin is therefore known everywhere as *Tursiops truncatus*; *Tursiops* (Latin and Greek 'face like a porpoise') refers to the genus or group of species that this animal belongs to: *truncatus* (Latin 'truncated') refers to the actual species within that group.

Although there remains a huge diversity of cetacean species, they can be broadly split into two groups: the mysticetes or baleen whales and the odontocetes or toothed whales. The baleen whales have enormous mouths filled with hundreds of plates made of baleen, a tough keratin-based material similar in nature to our own fingernails. These plates hang vertically from the roof of the mouth like a vertical Venetian blind and form a sieve. The whales feed by either straining or gulping huge quantities of water through the baleen plates to filter out the plankton, shrimp-like crustaceans and small fish which make up their diet.

The eleven species of baleen whales include some of the largest and most magnificent cetaceans. Sadly, the approachability and size of species such as the right and gray whales made them an easy target for early whalers. As these populations became depleted, more sophisticated boats and weaponry allowed the whaling industry to exploit the faster blue, fin and sei whales. Today, some of these populations are

Dolphins' nostrils are on top of their heads and they
only need to brush the water surface to snatch a breath of air.
Like Olympic swimmers, they exhale just before reaching the surface,
reducing the amount of time spent above the water
to a fraction of a second.

showing signs of recovery, and many are now the target of the growing whale-watching industry.

All other sixty-seven species of cetacean belong to the toothed whales or Odontocetes (Latin *dont,* 'teeth' and Latin and Greek *cetus/kétos,* 'whale'). Four main groupings of living odontocetes exist, each known as a superfamily. The first two contain the mysterious and little-known deep divers: the Physeteridae or sperm whales and the Ziphiidae or beaked and bottlenose whales. All twenty-one species live in deep waters and are believed to feed primarily on squid. The sperm whale, the best known of all, has been recorded to dive to over 3600 ft (1100 meters) and remain submerged for up to 90 minutes. Male sperm whales may travel the world's oceans in a lifetime, feeding in the high northern latitudes and mating with females living in warmer equatorial waters.

Despite our scientific endeavors, the beaked whales still remain a mystery to us. They are shy of boats and are rarely seen at sea, though they may be quite common. Some species have only been seen dead, found stranded on beaches or even discovered by scientists for sale in fish markets. It is remarkable to think that there may still be species of whale the size of a small yacht swimming in the oceans, influenced by our actions, but as yet unrecorded!

The third and most ancient superfamily of toothed whales is the Platanistoidea or river dolphins. All five representatives live in the world's major rivers and include species such as the Indus and Amazon river dolphins and other of the world's most endangered cetaceans. In these rivers, the water can be almost opaque and three of these species are almost blind, depending upon their sophisticated acoustic abilities to find food and to navigate around the river channels.

The Delphinoidea represent the widest assortment of species in terms of size, color and habits, from the brightly colored and agile common dolphins to those fearsome predators, the massive killer whales or orcas. The smallest species in this superfamily are the porpoises or Phoceonidae, growing to a little over 6 ft 6 in (2 meters) at most. This is a long-established cetacean family, but today it is represented by just six species. These include the harbor porpoise, commonly found in the North

Atlantic, with a blunt head and small spade-shaped teeth which are typical of the family. In complete dental contrast, the narwhal, with its long unicorn-like tusk, and the beluga or white whale, belong to the Monodontidae family. Finally, the Delphinidae family, 'true' dolphins, contains over thirty species, including the pilot and killer whales, and the striped, common, white-sided, Risso's and bottlenose dolphin.

No one can deny that the bottlenose dolphins have come a long way from their shrew-like ancestors. Their bodies are highly streamlined and shaped like elegant torpedoes and, in common with all other cetaceans, their skulls have changed radically from those of their land-based ancestors. The bones have telescoped so that the elongated jaws point forward to form a beak, each jaw containing up to 54 simple peg-like teeth. The nostrils have fused, and now open at the top of the head through a single opening known as the blow-hole. Where the body thickens behind the head, the dolphin's ancient fore-legs have become shrunken and, along with their 'fingers', form flippers. The hind legs have disappeared completely from view and only a few tiny bones remain, buried deep within the animal's sides. Massive muscles in the rear half of the body beat the sickle-shaped tail flukes up and down, propelling the dolphin at speeds of over 25 miles per hour (40 kmph). A fatty dorsal fin acts like a keel on a sailing boat, stabilizing the animal as it moves through the water. On its surface, there is little sign of its original mammalian hair. Instead, the skin is underlaid with a thick layer of blubber, serving the triple role of insulation, energy reserve, and giving the dolphins their characteristic streamlined form.

Many fossil remains of extinct dolphins from this family have been found, but we are still left with gaps in the story of how and where they evolved into their modern form. The earliest fossil species recognizable as a *Tursiops* was found in an old mine in North Carolina, in sediments deposited around five million years ago. Other specimens have been unearthed in both the Pacific and Atlantic basins, while many others originate from the Mediterranean region.

These discoveries suggest that the early *Tursiops* occurred over a very wide area, and this is reflected in the distribution of its modern descendants. Today, bottlenose dolphins

*Bottlenose dolphins live in a wide range of habitats, from
shallow coastal areas to oceanic waters.*

can be found throughout almost all of the world's temperate and tropical oceans and coastal waters. They occur as far north as Nova Scotia, Norway, northern California and northern Japan, and as far south as Chile and the southern tips of New Zealand, Argentina and South Africa.

This extensive range exposes them to an enormous variety of marine habitats, from shallow muddy inshore lagoons to deep oceans. In many of these areas, resident bottlenose dolphins have become specialized to suit the local conditions. As a result, we see a great variety of forms within this single species, with dolphins varying in their body size, behavior and color. For example, bottlenose dolphins are generally dark gray, charcoal or brown on their backs, gradually paling on their flanks to a pale cream or pink belly. The flippers and tail flukes are also dark gray, but many individuals are scratched and pale around their mouths or on the tip of their snouts. But there are some marked regional variations to this general color scheme. In the Red Sea, dolphins often display two or three diagonal bands on their tailstocks, whereas dolphins in the Indian Ocean develop a spot pattern on their bellies once they mature.

Some of these differences are so marked that it was once thought that there might be as many as twelve species of bottlenose dolphins. More recently, an extensive study of dolphins around the coast of Australia led to the conclusion that they are all members of one highly variable species. Bottlenose dolphins inhabiting Australia's cooler southern waters are large, while those living in tropical environments along the northern coast are small with proportionally larger flippers. The larger southern animals are better able to conserve heat, but the smaller animals in the north are more agile and maneuverable. These smaller animals may, however, overheat because fast swimming can generate excess heat. This might be a bonus in cold water, but in tropical waters the extra heat must be lost. The large flippers on these warm-water animals may therefore act as radiators, releasing heat from the blood into the surrounding water when necessary.

It is perhaps not surprising that such marked differences in body form led people to believe that they were dealing with two different species. However, after inspecting dolphins from around the entire Australian coast, it was discovered that the size of the dolphins' bodies and fins changed gradually. Furthermore, these changes were related to differences in local water temperatures, suggesting that bottlenose dolphins have adapted to a wide range of environmental conditions.

In other cases, two distinct forms of bottlenose dolphin are found in approximately the same area. Off the coast of South Africa and off the southeastern coast of the U.S.A., there co-exist a small form, the so-called 'coastal ecotype', and a larger form, the 'offshore ecotype'. The coastal animals are similar to those seen in northern Australia, whilst those living offshore resemble the larger animals from colder waters in the south. Given the explanations of the Australian study, how do these two forms occur in the same latitudes? The answer again appears to be related to their differing habitat. The small animals live in shallow waters, while the larger offshore dolphins are generally found in waters of around 650 ft (200 meters) in depth over the edge of the continental shelf.

According to the Australian studies we might expect the water temperatures of these areas to be different, but this does not seem to be the case. Nevertheless, other factors explain the differences in these dolphins' body sizes and shapes. Offshore animals have different blood characteristics, giving them a greater ability to store oxygen. They also appear to feed on fish and squid which occur only in deep water. To catch these prey, offshore dolphins have to dive to great depths, explaining the specialized blood chemistry which permits them to make long dives. Large body size also increases an animal's diving ability, while the temperature of these deep waters is also much cooler. Together, these two facts help explain why larger animals are more successful in the offshore areas. In the chilly waters around the British Isles it is not surprising to find that only one type of dolphin can survive, and this area has produced some of the largest recorded bottlenose dolphins.

Having a body that is suited to a specific temperature is all very well, but, like the land, the seas have seasons, and water temperatures in an area may change. To compensate for this, dolphins store up or draw upon their blubber layer, changing its insulating properties in relation to the season.

An alternative option is to migrate, and this is what some bottlenose dolphins on the

east coast of the U.S.A. do each year, moving north in the warm summer months and returning south in the winter.

Bottlenose dolphins occupy a diverse range of habitats: from the deep oceans to quiet shallow lagoons, from muddy estuaries to exposed coral reefs, even into the lower reaches of rivers. These varied habitats bring with them a variety of water qualities, predators and fish communities. Some habitats may support large groups of dolphins, while in others a few individuals may have to struggle to make a living. In some places it may pay animals to stay in a small area which they get to know intimately. Individual coastal bottlenose dolphins certainly appear to have strong affinities with particular areas, living together in groups which may inhabit the same home range for generations. In the waters of the Gulf of Mexico, almost the whole coastline is home for many thousands of dolphins. This continuum is broken up, however, into a patchwork of different local communities.

Bottlenose dolphins around the British Isles also appear to favor certain coastal areas, but the animals are much less common and they have concentrated themselves into just a few distinct areas. In contrast, offshore and migratory groups may range much more extensively.

This widespread distribution makes bottlenose dolphins an ideal subject for us to investigate how differences in an animal's environment shape its behavior and ecology. The studies in Australia illustrated how comparing dolphins from areas of differing water temperature helped explain variations in body form. Similarly, comparative studies can tell us whether the presence of predators may affect dolphin social behavior, or whether differences in the distribution of food supplies determine whether a group remains in one area or wanders the oceans.

Our own activities may also alter the animals' environment and behavior. An understanding of how dolphin populations respond to natural environmental changes can therefore help us understand how best to protect their habitats and conserve their populations.

Adaptation to local conditions has resulted in physical differences in bottlenose dolphins from Scotland (top) and Australia (bottom).

The Search for Food

The thrill of seeing a group of dolphins surging across the surface of the water after a school of fish, predators and prey flying in all directions, is something which is almost impossible to convey in words. Even the remarkable still and video pictures now available fail to capture completely the atmosphere of close encounters with dolphins. To researchers, the spectacular variety of feeding techniques used by dolphins makes the study of their foraging behavior particularly exciting. What is frustrating, however, is that most of this feeding behavior occurs below the surface, out of sight.

What is clear is that bottlenose dolphins employ a range of feeding techniques which more than match the diversity of habitats in which they live. In narrow tidal creeks in Georgia and South Carolina, for example, dolphins chase fish onto mudflats and temporarily beach themselves to pick their prey from the shore. Elsewhere in the Gulf of Mexico, they are regularly seen capturing fish by 'fish-whacking'; flicking them up to thirty feet in the air with their tail flukes. They then swim over to the stunned and wounded fish, and pick it easily from the surface of the water.

It is while feeding that co-operation between members of a group is particularly dramatic. In the inshore waters of the Moray Firth in Scotland, we often see dolphins feeding on salmon returning to Highland rivers to breed. Salmon are large and fast, and the dolphins often need to work together to catch them. At times we have watched a group of three or four individuals diving in a close circle, apparently herding salmon. On occasions, our suspicions have been confirmed dramatically, as a dolphin dashes through the centre of the group with a salmon in its jaws.

Many people are aware of the concept of close co-operation between members of a dolphin group. More surprising is the fact that bottlenose dolphins are one of the few animal species to have developed a symbiotic feeding relationship with humans. Early visitors to the south-eastern coast of Australia recorded scenes in

*Foraging activity can be exciting to watch, but understanding
exactly how and where dolphins feed can be a frustrating and difficult
task. Prey is often caught below the surface so we know little about
the food requirements of most bottlenose dolphin populations.*

which Aborigines would slap the surface of the water with their spears on seeing a school of mullet. Dolphins then drove the mullet before them, towards the shore, and the Aborigines dashed into the water with spears and handnets to catch some of the fish. In Mauritania, coastal communities still fish in this way.

An even more complex form of co-operation exists around the town of Laguna on the southern tip of Brazil. Here, highly ritualized co-operative fishing takes place between a community of 30 to 40 fishermen and resident groups of dolphins. The fishermen stand in the shallow murky water poised with their circular throw nets while one or two dolphins station themselves a few yards out to sea. From time to time the dolphins casually submerge, but the fishermen wait for the specific moment when a dolphin makes an abrupt stereotyped surface roll. At this point, the men cast their nets and the fish are either caught under the weighted rim of the net or become tangled in the mesh. Meanwhile the dolphins take

Dolphins sometimes play with their prey.

advantage of the confusion amongst the shoal of fish, snatching those escaping from the nets. The technique provides great benefits for both humans and dolphins; as a result these learned behaviors have persisted for generations of both species.

Less spectacular, but equally important for some groups of dolphins, are feeding behaviors that have developed around commercial trawlers. Good examples are found around the shrimp boats of the Gulf of Mexico and the Australian coast. Dolphins patrol behind fishing boats, either capturing fish which escape from the trawl or waiting for fishermen to throw discarded fish overboard. In some cases, dolphins may even hang around fishing boats at anchor after the day's work, feeding upon fish which are attracted to the debris falling from the nets or pumped from the bilges.

In concentrating upon these more obvious feeding behaviors there is, however, a danger that our impression of the diet of bottlenose dolphins becomes biased towards those fish which are captured at the surface. This is probably why so many researchers have recorded surface-dwelling mullet as an important prey item. In many areas though, feeding takes place below the surface. For example, we have often seen dolphins repeatedly surfacing in the narrow channels of the inner Moray Firth, remaining stationed into the oncoming tide, or in deeper water, a series of short dives may be followed by a steep arched roll as the dolphin raises its tail fluke before disappearing for a minute or two to feed at depth.

Obtaining a more representative picture of what dolphins eat presents real problems. We cannot easily follow their tracks and collect the fecal samples which underpin so many feeding studies of mammals and birds on land. Instead, our only representative information on their food comes from the few areas where large numbers of animals have been stranded or caught either accidentally or intentionally, allowing the examination of the dolphins' stomach contents. The picture emerging from these studies is again one of marked variability, with the nature of the dolphins' diet differing according to local conditions and habits. Unlike sperm or pilot whales, bottlenose dolphins feed on a wide range of fish species, as well as cephalopods such as squid and octopus.

Information on the habits of these prey species can also tell us which underwater habitats the dolphins feed in. For example, off the coast of South Africa some dolphins were caught in nets set to keep sharks from bathing beaches. These animals had eaten over seventy-two types of prey, including fish which live on sandy bottom habitats, others from inshore reefs, and both fish and squid which form large schools in deep waters offshore. It therefore seems likely that every population of bottlenose dolphins will have a slightly different diet depending upon which fish or squid are to be found locally.

Of more interest are questions relating to how dolphins locate and choose their prey in a particular area. Do they prefer to seek out certain fish species, or do they

*Dolphins often hunt in packs, co-ordinating their actions
to round up and chase schools of fish.*

*In some clear tropical waters, dolphin feeding techniques
may be observed by scuba-divers. This dolphin can be seen
digging a series of craters in an attempt to catch prey
which has buried itself in the sandy bottom.*

simply feed on any fish they happen to encounter on their travels? One factor likely to affect their choice from the menu is the energy content of the potential meal. Estimates of the food requirements of cetaceans are notoriously difficult to make. Nevertheless, studies in captivity indicate that bottlenose dolphins must eat 3 to 6 per cent of their body weight each day, more if they are lactating females. For a dolphin weighing over 66 lb (300 kg) that is a lot of food to catch, and it would be advantageous to reduce the number of individual fish required by selecting food with a high energy content. On this basis, richer herring or salmon would be a better choice than whiting or flounder of equivalent size.

However, there is no such thing as a free meal – even for a dolphin. The spectacular nature of some feeding behaviors inevitably means that they are energetically costly. There is no point in chasing a large fat fish if a dolphin uses up more energy trying to catch it than is gained by eating it. Choosing prey is therefore a balancing act between the cost of catching and digesting different species or sizes of fish and the benefits that each meal offers. As a consequence, low-quality prey, like flat fish, may sometimes feature in the diet if those prey are also easy to catch.

Another potential cost when feeding is the possibility that the prey will retaliate. Many dolphins in Florida carry fish spines embedded in their tail flukes; presumably the final calling card of an unfortunate fish as it was 'fish-whacked' into the air. Some fish are also venomous, and observations around Australian shrimp boats suggest that dolphins avoid taking these species when they are discarded from the trawl.

Bottlenose dolphins have good eyesight both above and below water, and can catch fish by sight alone. The sea, however, is often far from clear; rivers and wave-action can make coastal waters almost opaque. Marine animals living and moving around in these low-visibility environments therefore have to use other senses to find food. Many, especially those which live around the sea bottom, orientate themselves by touch. Others which move around in the water column use vibrations. Fish, for example, use their lateral-line network of sensory pores to sense the vibrations coming from an approaching predator or fleeing prey.

Bottlenose dolphins, like other toothed whales, use a similar but rather more sophisticated system for obtaining information on their environment. Instead of sensing vibrations with a lateral line, they listen with their inner ears. As well as listening passively to the sounds around them, such as the crashing of surf on a headland or the whine of a boat engine, dolphins actively make noises. The resulting echoes help them build up a highly detailed picture of their surrounding environment. This 'echolocation' technique is also used by bats and the principle has been utilized by humans, in the sonar systems of boats and submarines.

Dolphins are experts at this technique. Blindfolded, they can swim easily around pools, pick up fish and discriminate between objects of different shape or density without being able to see or touch them. When echolocating they make extremely brief and very loud clicking noises in the airways in their heads. The dished shape of their skulls helps to reflect these sounds forward, through a domed mass of fatty tissue on the front of the dolphin's head, called the melon. This tissue acts like a lens and focuses the clicks into a narrow beam of sound that projects directly in front of the dolphin. As a click travels through the water, the sound waves hit objects in their path; a fish, a rocky wall, or even another dolphin. These objects will then bounce some of that sound back to the dolphin, which picks up the sound through its lower jaws, which then conduct it to the inner ear.

The amount and pitch of the sound reaching the dolphin provides information on the nature of the object. And since sound takes time to travel through water, the delay can be used to estimate the distance between the dolphin and the object. Because of this time delay, a dolphin cannot click continuously. Instead, it waits for each click to be reflected back before it makes the next. The more distant the object, the longer the waves take to complete their journey, and so the slower the dolphin clicks.

A hunting dolphin sounds rather like a fishing reel or bicycle wheel clicking around. As the dolphin approaches its prey, the journey time for the sound gets shorter. The dolphin can then click faster and faster, producing a 'mew' which sounds rather like a door creaking. Consequently, we can learn much about feeding

Dolphins seek an easy meal around trawlers (top).
A lone adult dives down to feed at depth (bottom).

behavior by listening to dolphins when they are underwater. Steady or occasional clicking indicates that they are looking for food or monitoring their environment. Lots of echolocation, mews and buzzing indicates that they are chasing prey.

Although echolocation is highly efficient at ranges of less than 330 ft (100 meters), dolphins must use other skills to find prey over longer distances. Dolphins often appear to return to the same areas to feed at certain stages of the tidal cycle or times of year, presumably when fish are plentiful. A good memory for these potential feeding sites, perhaps partly learned during the long association with their mothers, is probably one factor allowing them to effectively exploit areas of fluctuating food availability. Nevertheless, occasional unpredictable changes in the environment have shown how quickly bottlenose dolphins can respond to changes in the distribution of their food. Some of the richest feeding areas for marine predators are found in the Pacific Ocean, where cold currents rise to the surface off the coast of South America. Every few years, however, climatic abnormalities lead to a change in current patterns and some food supplies decrease suddenly under these 'El Niño' conditions.

In 1983, a particularly severe 'El Niño' occurred. Many seabirds, fur seals and sea lions died as a result of the food shortage around the Galapagos Islands and along the Peruvian coast, and more subtle effects were felt as far north as California. It was here that a group of bottlenose dolphins, previously thought to have been resident off San Diego, showed how adaptable the species can be to such changes. As warm water and the dolphins' potential prey moved northward, several groups of dolphins moved with them. Over the next two to three months they swam over 400 miles (650 km) to Monterey Bay. As normal conditions returned, some animals traveled south, whilst others have remained in the Monterey Bay area.

This event illustrates how groups can overcome short-term food shortages by migrating in search of better supplies, and that environmental fluctuations of this kind can lead to changes in the geographical range of bottlenose dolphins.

A dolphin may leap out of the water
while feeding, playing or during sexual displays.
But look away for a moment and you
are sure to miss it!

Even when you see bottlenose dolphins they often leave you guessing what they are up to.

Life and Death in a Dolphin Society

Aspects of bottlenose dolphins' reproductive and social life vary, like their feeding behavior, according to differences in their local environment. The age at which they become sexually mature may differ depending upon the speed at which the young dolphins grow. In turn, these growth rates probably depend upon the amount, type or distribution of food in the area. Ironically, much of this information on the life-history of a dolphin becomes available only once the animal has died.

Stranded or accidentally caught dolphins can yield information on diet, but much more can be learned from the study of dead animals. A tooth, carefully sectioned, provides an estimate of the age of the animal, the growth layers in the tooth being laid down annually like the rings of a tree. Knowledge of the animal's age can then be combined with measurements of its length and weight to estimate how fast it grew. Examination of the ovaries or testes can tell us whether a female had recently calved or whether a male of a certain age was capable of fathering a calf. In addition, a detailed post-mortem may shed light on the cause of the dolphin's death.

In recent years, our understanding of the biology of living dolphins has improved greatly through the long-term study of individuals. Many dolphins bear unique nicks in their dorsal fins, or body-scars from encounters with other dolphins or their predators. Using these natural marks, we can identify individuals from photographs, just as pictures of unique pigmentation patterns have been used to recognize individual humpback and killer whales.

These 'photo-identification techniques' can be used to study many aspects of cetacean biology. For example, repeated observations of the same dolphin can show how individuals move around, while systematic photographic surveys give an indication of the size of dolphin populations. Such studies can also provide information on population characteristics which could previously only be estimated from dead dolphins. By following individual females over many years we can discover how often they give birth and whether there is any difference in calving rates between young and old females. Regular observations of calves can also show how long the youngsters remain with their mothers and, eventually, at what age they themselves start to breed.

One of the longest and most detailed studies of this kind has been undertaken in Sarasota Bay, Florida. Over the last 30 years or so, this work has provided information which underpins our understanding of the dynamics of bottlenose dolphin populations. Furthermore, the results have encouraged ourselves and many others to carry out similar studies of dolphins in contrasting environments. However, some of the dolphins which have been followed in Sarasota Bay are nearly twice as old as the study. Research on such long-lived animals can take many years to produce results, and it may be a long time before detailed comparisons can be made between bottlenose dolphins in different areas. Consequently, our picture of the life of a bottlenose dolphin is based very heavily on Sarasota animals, with additional information on particular aspects of their biology coming from a variety of other studies of live, dead and captive dolphins.

Our knowledge of the behavior of pregnant bottlenose dolphins and of mothers with young calves is based largely upon observation of captive animals. Their labor is very short, often only lasting for twenty minutes or so, with the calf generally emerging tail first. This brief labor, and the tendency for births in captivity to occur at night, means that the chances of anyone being lucky enough to witness the event in the wild are extremely slim. In captivity calves can be born in any month, whereas our observations of dolphins off the Scottish coast suggest that most births occur in the late summer. Other studies of wild populations have also found that youngsters appear in particular seasons, but the timing of births varies between studies and has probably evolved in each area to avoid seasons when predators are abundant, when food is in short supply or when water temperatures are unfavorable. Similarly, pregnant females may move into certain areas to give birth, particularly to avoid predators such as sharks.

At birth, calves are a little under 3 ft (1 meter) long. They can swim immediately

*Close friends or just temporary acquaintances? Long term studies are
just beginning to show the patterns of dolphin society.*

Mothers and calves stay close. Separation in the first few months of life would mean certain death for the calf.

and are usually able to make their own way to the surface to take their first breath. Within an hour or so of birth, the calf will suckle from the pair of teats which are usually concealed in slits in the mother's belly. For the first week or so, these feeds are short and frequent, occurring up to four times an hour. At this time, young calves can be recognized easily in the wild, both by their appearance and their behavior. Not only are newborn calves much paler than adults and juveniles but they also have marked vertical lines, or 'fetal folds', on their flanks. Bottlenose dolphin calves are large in relation to the size of the mother, and these folds are thought to be a result of the calf being crumpled up in the mother's womb.

Their behavior at the surface is also distinctive, with the calves breathing shortly after their mother, rushing out of the water as if afraid that they are about to be left behind. Underwater, the calf remains close to, often touching, its mother's flank. This allows it to save energy by hitching a ride on the vacuum produced as the female moves through the water. In this position the pair's color patterns also coalesce, blending the two animals together and making the vulnerable newborn calf less obvious to visual predators.

As the calf is so dependent on its mother for food and protection, it is clear that the pair must stay in close contact. To maintain this bond, mothers and calves call to each other or, more specifically, whistle. When the youngster is first born, the mother whistles, over and over again, a specific whistle which we call a signature whistle. Each bottlenose dolphin has its own whistle which is different in tone, form and duration from any other dolphin's. To our ears, signature whistles are high-pitched, crisp notes which can sweep up or down in frequency. Whistles can last between a fraction of, to more than a second. These high-pitched sounds can be heard above the lower background noise of their underwater world. So once a young dolphin has learnt the characteristics of its mother's whistle it will always be able to find her, even among a large school of other mothers and their calves.

Similarly, the calf develops a signature whistle which will allow it to be recognized by its mother and other members of the local community. But, just as

Bow-riders: a school of torpedo-like dolphins ride the immense
pressure wave in front of a ship, like a gang of surfers.

*Bottlenose dolphins are rarely shy and will approach unfamiliar
objects in the water. As well as bow-riding they will often swim around
and alongside boats for many miles. They have been observed doing the
same with large whales, perhaps escorting or cheekily hitching
a ride on the great animal's pressure wave.*

human babies are unable to make precise noises, young dolphins have to go through a long period of practicing and perfecting their whistles. The youngster eventually learns a distinctive whistle which it will continue to use throughout its life.

Many of the other skills essential in adulthood also require gradual development and practice. As a result, the calf is dependent upon its mother for an extensive period, although the nature of this relationship gradually changes. As the youngster grows older, suckling is concentrated into fewer and longer bouts. The mother's milk has a fat content of around 14 per cent, over four times that of human or cow's milk, and the calf grows rapidly during its first year of life.

At around six months old, the milk feeds are supplemented with solid food which the calf may capture itself or be given by its mother. As it grows more proficient at feeding its dependence upon its mother declines, but it may continue to take the occasional meal of milk until it is several years old. As they are more than capable of catching all their own food, it seems unlikely that suckling is essential to these older animals for nutrition. Amongst the toothed whales and dolphins, such behavior may therefore have a role in maintaining social bonds. This could explain why adult male sperm whales have been found with milk in their stomachs and why female pilot whales, who had not given birth for many years, have been found to be producing milk.

This bond between mother and calf is the closest that we see in dolphin societies, but the pair do not behave in isolation. Bottlenose dolphins are sometimes found alone, but they are generally highly social animals and usually live in groups of anything from two or three individuals up to several hundred.

As a result of the intensive photo-identification studies in Sarasota Bay, the nature of these dolphins' social life is best understood for coastal groups from these shallow waters. Here, the average school size is around seven, but the composition of these schools is very fluid. If you followed any group for a day or so, the individuals present in it would change. Nonetheless, if the comings and goings of dolphins in these schools are watched over a much longer period, a pattern gradually emerges.

Dolphins spend most of their lives underwater. A brief glimpse at the surface is often all we get.

In Sarasota Bay, females of similar reproductive state tend to swim together in groups known as bands. Some bands include mothers with young calves while others consist predominantly of pregnant females. A calf, therefore, grows up in a group containing animals of a similar age. As they become more independent from their mothers, these youngsters interact increasingly both with each other and with passing boats. In the Moray Firth, we've found that these animals of one or two years old are the keenest to come over and bow-ride during our surveys, sometimes racing along and distracting us for ten minutes or more.

Eventually, when they are between about three and six years old, the youngsters will leave their maternal group. Juvenile dolphins of both sexes join together and form sub-adult herds, fending for themselves for the first time. It is a difficult period in their lives and many young dolphins die at this stage. In these groups, young dolphins have to develop and practice many of their social skills: fights, sexual activity, chasing and leaping are often observed.

While this very active social behavior can been seen at the surface, a huge range of extraordinary vocalizations can be heard underwater. Words are woefully inadequate to convey the variety of these strange sounds, but they range from clucks to squawks, wails, croaks and barks. These sounds are made up of many echolocation clicks in quick succession. Known as burst pulse sounds, their exact function is unknown, but it has been suggested that they are used predominantly in social settings. Divers who have been in the water while dolphins are making these noises say that they can feel the noises as much as they hear them. This is not surprising as the clicks are extremely intense and focused into a narrow beam to the front of the dolphin. Divers have also reported seeing vocalizing dolphins swimming with their beaks almost touching the belly or side of another animal. Perhaps they are using their echolocation system to assess the physical state of the other animal? Or the power in the clicks may even be being used as a form of massage!

Young dolphins stay in these bachelor groups until they become sexually mature. For a female bottlenose dolphin, this may occur as early as seven or eight

At four years old this Scottish dolphin may soon leave its mother's
company to join animals of a similar age.

years old, and she may produce her first calf after a twelve-month gestation period. Around the time when her calf is born she will return to her mother's band, joining her sisters, aunts and even grandmothers. But although she may be mature enough to mate and conceive, she is not yet fully grown and this may lead to difficulties during late pregnancy or labor. Based on detailed studies of more easily observed mammals, the success of these younger females' attempts at motherhood are likely to be poor. Even if they successfully give birth to their firstborn, their inexperience may subsequently affect the calf's chances of survival.

The problems faced by young mothers may also affect their own health, and this is likely to select against those females which reproduce too early. As a result, most female bottlenose dolphins do not become mature until they are around eleven or twelve years old. After this they may produce a calf every two to four years; sooner if the previous calf dies or longer if their current calf is slow to grow and reach independence. In 1990 we saw several adult females from one Moray Firth band with young calves, but one of the youngsters disappeared and presumably died when it was only six months old. Eighteen months later, its mother produced another calf, but her companions were still rearing the surviving calves and had not yet given birth again. This reproductive cycle may continue for 20 or 30 years, with females of over 40 years old being seen with young calves in the Sarasota study.

The fine details of the dolphins' sex-lives remain a mystery. However, it does appear that males have at least two strategies when they mature and leave the sub-adult herd. Some may go off on their own, while others team up with one or two males of a similar age, often close relatives or old companions. These small alliances of males move around together for many years, traveling from one female band to another, searching for receptive females. Their association with any particular female is therefore brief and males play no part in helping to rear the young.

In Western Australia, one group of bottlenose dolphins living in the clear waters of Shark Bay has become used to being hand fed by the tourists who visit the bay. This situation has allowed the close observation of these male alliances and has shown how different alliances can compete very strongly with each other. One pair of males can separate out a receptive female from her band, monopolize her for several days, and frequently attempt to mate with her. However, the success of these mating attempts, and the degree of choice that females retain in choosing which males they mate with, remain uncertain. While the female is being guarded, other male alliances may try to capture her, and these conflicts can lead to violent head-to-head fights and chases. If one male alliance fails to capture a female, they may even

Calves are much paler than adults.

join forces with another pair. This may improve their chances of fathering more offspring, but the stresses and dangers involved in these mating activities mean that males are less likely to survive as long as the females; 25 to 35 years being considered old for a male compared with the 40+ years possible for a female.

In Shark Bay a whole group of dolphins have become habituated to humans but in many instances single dolphins also seek human company. These wild sociable dolphins do not generally seem to be soliciting food. Instead their relationship with humans appears to center around play behavior, often with extensive physical contact. In many cases these animals are old males.

Around the British and Irish coasts, where sightings of dolphins can be scarce, two such animals have not only become famous but also made a major contribution to the local economy. One, known as Fungi, has been resident around the Dingle Peninsula off the west coast of Ireland since the late 1980s. In Northumberland, another male called Freddy spent almost all his time within a few miles of the small

Local differences in the dolphins' underwater environment may influence their behavior and social patterns.

town of Amble from 1987 until he disappeared mysteriously in 1992.

It is unclear why some dolphins should choose to befriend humans in this way. Some old males may be social outcasts but other reports involve younger animals of both sexes. Whatever the reason for such behavior, these individuals often provide people with a memorable first encounter with dolphins.

We are unlikely ever to know what finally happened to Freddy or sociable dolphins like him, whether he eventually joined another wild group of dolphins or simply died and disappeared without trace. It is difficult to find out how and when wild dolphins die. Some dead dolphins are washed up on beaches but these animals are often too decomposed for us to be able to discover the major causes of death in this species. In fact the final cause of death may often be misleading, simply being the manifestation of a more serious underlying problem. An animal that dies in a collision with a boat may already have been debilitated by a disease which made it prone to remain at the surface for long periods. Similarly, dolphins taken by sharks or other predators may already be in a poor condition. Although examinations of stranded animals have recorded a whole range of bacterial, viral and fungal infections, it is unclear whether many of these organisms have important implications for the health of wild dolphins.

One feature of marine mammal populations which has recently been discovered is that these species suffer from occasional mass mortalities, when unusually high numbers of dead animals are found within a short period. In 1990, over four hundred Mediterranean striped dolphins died as the result of a distemper virus infection similar to one which affected North Sea seals a few years previously. It has since been shown that bottlenose dolphins also carry antibodies to the same or a similar virus but, so far, there has been no evidence of any of these dolphins dying from distemper.

There have been recent mass deaths of bottlenose dolphins which have been attributed to other causes. The largest of these occurred in the winter of 1987 when over 750 dolphins were reported dead along the southeastern coast of the U.S.A.

As for other mass mortalities, the media and pressure groups were quick to cite pollution as the primary cause of the deaths. Inevitably, the situation was much more complex than this, and an extensive study for the United States Marine Mammal Commission concluded that the dolphins had died from eating fish which contained naturally occurring brevotoxins. Brevotoxins are produced by small planktonic algae which can form 'red tides' in certain conditions, and also cause health problems in humans. It was suggested that the toxins had suppressed the dolphins' immune systems, thus making them vulnerable to a range of other diseases.

Dolphins are easily maimed by propellers.

These conclusions remain controversial. Critics highlighted the fact that tests for brevotoxins were made only on a small number of the dolphins; and that fewer than half of these had proved positive. In particular they noted that high levels of pollutants were found in many dead animals and that these too may affect the immune system.

More recent studies have uncovered evidence of distemper virus infections in the tissues of the stranded dolphins, and agreement on the cause for the death of these dolphins may never be reached. Nevertheless, this and similar events have taught us much about the role of disease in the lives and deaths of marine mammals.

*Although it is hard to judge intelligence, we know that dolphins are
quick learners, have good memories and a sense of humor.*

Dolphin Conservation and Politics

The bottlenose dolphins' coastal habits bring them into close contact with humans in many parts of the world. In some areas this has led to dolphins being exploited for food, or worse still, as bait for obtaining a more valuable catch. In other places and cultures they have been regarded as messengers of the gods, and many peoples still consider dolphins to have mystical powers or special human virtues. Between these extremes there are many different levels of interaction between humans and dolphins.

In many cases the relationship is direct, such as in the co-operative fishing techniques used in Brazil or the use of trained dolphins by the United States Navy for military activities. In others, the potential impact of our own activities on the health of the dolphin populations is more subtle, notably where our activities lead to the deterioration of their environment. As consumers we buy products manufactured in factories which discharge industrial waste into the sea. Many of us eat fish caught using techniques which, even if 'dolphin friendly', still have an impact upon the marine environment. A greater understanding of the range of such threats facing dolphins today can help us discover how we can all, even as individuals, help alleviate these problems.

Directed hunting of small cetaceans is not carried out in the waters of most Western countries. Nevertheless, coastal communities from many other areas kill bottlenose dolphins either for food or because they are perceived to be competing for local fish stocks. Declines in commercial whaling have increased pressure on small cetaceans in Japanese waters, where species such as Dall's porpoise and bottlenose dolphin are hunted for meat. Bottlenose dolphins are also caught off the coast of South America, where their meat can be a significant source of protein for some of the world's poorest communities.

Dolphins are killed accidentally in fisheries directed at a variety of fish species. Because they live in inshore waters where obstacles are commonplace, bottlenose dolphins are probably less likely to blunder into nets than oceanic dolphins and porpoises. Nevertheless some individuals do become entangled in drift nets and trawls, and bottlenose dolphins can be found amongst the large schools of spinner and spotted dolphins which are sometimes caught by the tuna fishery in the eastern tropical Pacific. Heavy fishing in some areas may also affect dolphins by depleting their potential food supplies or by damaging the underwater habitats upon which they depend.

Occasional deaths may also result from collisions with boats. In areas such as Florida, where there is heavy powerboat traffic, animals can be seen with wounds and scars from propeller injuries. Freddy, the friendly dolphin from Northumberland, was hit by a boat in 1991, narrowly missing a fatal injury. As well as the problem of direct collisions, there has been growing concern over the effect of disturbance by boat traffic. Boats may directly disturb dolphins if, for example, they persistently follow mothers with young calves. However, most attention has focused on the problem of noise, particularly from powerful outboard motors or jetskis, which may interfere with the dolphins' social calls or echolocation systems. Recreational water sports are becoming more popular in many areas, and the rise in interest in dolphins themselves will increase the number of people wishing to take to the water to see the animals at close quarters.

The challenge for those who manage coastal areas is to facilitate the enjoyment of seeing wild dolphins without causing harm to the animals themselves. In principle, this should be possible by encouraging boat users to follow simple codes of conduct, especially avoiding high speed travel and sudden changes in direction while in the vicinity of dolphins. In many areas, people can also be encouraged to watch from the shore where good views of dolphins can be obtained, and any risk of disturbance or injury avoided.

Our habit of using the seas to dispose of many of our waste products underlies problems which are more complex to understand and more difficult to deal with. Water currents can carry pollutants over hundreds of miles; consequently, even if animals are known to be affected by pollution it may not be clear where the problem originated. This is especially true for persistent chemicals such as organochlorines, which include the insecticide DDT, and polychlorinated biphenyls (PCBs), which are used in many industrial processes. Concern has often been concentrated on these pollutants because they dissolve well in fat and can therefore build up to high levels in the blubber of marine mammals. Because they do not break down easily, organochlorines may also be passed on from generation to generation when

The bottlenose dolphins' coastal habits bring them into close contact with humans. In some areas they are hunted for food or killed to reduce perceived competition with fisheries. Elsewhere the potential threats are more subtle and poorly understood.

*Effective conservation policies require a better understanding
of the key threats which face bottlenose dolphins. This is one of many
individuals from the Moray Firth in Scotland with a gruesome skin condition,
but we do not yet know if this is a natural disease or related to pollution.
Further study is clearly required to address these questions.*

*In the meantime, we should not wait for such research before
we take positive action to improve the state of our seas. Dolphin and human
communities all depend upon a clean and productive marine environment
and we can all help to promote the wise use of this valuable resource.*

hungry calves cause their mothers to draw upon stored fat reserves to produce sufficient milk. Analyses of dolphin tissues have confirmed that organochlorines can be found in many individuals. Tests on one bottlenose dolphin from the Californian coast produced some of the highest organochlorine levels ever recorded in a cetacean.

Studies of other species have shown that these pollutants can reduce both male and female fertility and it is now widely believed that they may compromise the dolphins' ability to fight off disease. The effects of pollution are therefore confused with many other factors such as disease and malnutrition, and are difficult to identify without the most detailed of studies. Many people believe that governments should therefore adopt the precautionary principle. In other words, measures should be taken to decrease overall discharges of pollutants without waiting for concrete evidence to link a particular source of these chemicals to a particular problem.

Other types of pollution are more localized, for example the contamination caused by the sewage which we discharge or dump around our coasts. Sewage effluent can contain high levels of heavy metals and other industrial contaminants, and dolphins may also be vulnerable to human pathogens. The impacts of oil pollution often tend to be focused upon birds, but dolphins may also be affected by spills of crude oil or lighter petroleum compounds such as diesel. Observations around recent oil slicks have shown that dolphins do not avoid these areas, and their inhalation of toxic vapors could lead to chronic health problems.

The dramatic nature of the direct and indirect kills of dolphins and whales has led to a high level of public concern about the destructive impact we may be having on these animals. As a result of public, media and governmental pressure there are now international and national agreements which aim to promote the conservation of cetaceans.

Bottlenose dolphins are listed under the new European Union Habitats Directive, and special areas of conservation have been identified to protect the habitats of these and other key wildlife species. Because of their wide-ranging habits, cetaceans are also protected under the Bonn Convention, an agreement concerned with those species which travel widely over the boundaries of different nations. Governments have subsequently responded to these international agreements with domestic legislation, and national laws in many countries require the complete protection of bottlenose dolphins and other small cetaceans.

Nevertheless, despite these good intentions, there are few signs of positive action aimed at conserving dolphin populations. In many cases this is not surprising, given our lack of understanding of so many aspects of the ecology of bottlenose dolphins in many areas. Effective conservation policies depend upon a sound understanding of the populations we wish to conserve and the nature of the threats which face them. How can we hope to protect the dolphins' food supply if we do not know what they eat?

Similarly, we can outline the range of potential threats which their populations face, but our limited information on the precise nature of these threats constrains efforts to decide which of them are most significant. Indeed, there is often disagreement over what factors make a particular threat significant. Direct kills such as those seen during the Faroese pilot whale hunt are of concern on welfare and ethical grounds. However, they may be insignificant in conservation terms because the level of hunting is probably sustainable and unlikely to lead to a reduction in population size. It is the issues involving individual suffering, animal welfare and moral questions which tend to attract most media and public concern. Many conservation biologists and managers argue that more attention should be paid to those less obvious activities which act at the population level; altering the dynamics or behavior of the population rather than just affecting a few individuals.

Welfare issues are clearly important but, if we are concerned about conserving dolphin populations, action and limited resources need to be targeted at the wider problems. Although our attempts are often constrained by our scientific understanding, the issues are further clouded by cultural and political factors. For example, most of the countries pressing for international agreements to protect cetaceans have stopped killing dolphins or whales for human consumption. Politically then, it is much easier to focus attention on stopping other nations hunting dolphins and whales than the more uncomfortable process of tackling the wider problems like pollution or over-fishing. These require a closer, more demanding look at our own behavior; both as nations and as individuals.

Getting Involved

Despite the popular misconception, you do not have to sail across an ocean to see wild dolphins. Bottlenose dolphins can be seen in the most unlikely of places: amongst the surf crashing onto a beach, in estuaries and around harbors. With a little detective work, patience and a keen eye it is not at all difficult to see these magnificent creatures in the wild.

For those who wish to take to water, try one of the many 'whale watching' trips which have sprung up around the world. Trips range from brief excursions lasting an hour or two to adventurous voyages of a week of more. The industry has gone through a meteoric explosion in recent years. Unfortunately, some operators think about their revenue before the animals; so try to pick a recommended charter, find out if there are local guidelines for boat conduct and look for educational material on board. Most importantly if you feel that the boat is harassing the animals do not be afraid to say so.

For those who want to get even closer, there are many dolphins in captivity, particularly in the United States. There are also several places where people can swim with and even touch wild or semi-wild bottlenose dolphins. Again, remember your responsibilities and treat them with respect; even so-called 'friendly' dolphins are not immune to mood swings.

Enjoying seeing dolphins is one thing, but many people also want to help them. There are numerous organizations that are devoted to improving the future for dolphins and whales. Indeed most of the world's research and political lobbying on this subject is directly funded by charitable donations. Find out where your money is going and be selective, there are plenty to choose from.

Because of limited funds most research projects also rely on the help of dedicated volunteers. There are a growing number of activity holidays where people can gain experience of research work while directly and financially aiding the projects. Even casual sightings of dolphins can be of great benefit to scientific research, and there are several schemes which collect this information from the public. For the very keen, such voluntary work can lead to a career in this area.

Whatever your level of interest, everybody can help protect the marine environment by acting on a personal level. Find out where your waste goes, where foods such as tuna have come from, and where necessary lobby your local government. Politicians ultimately answer to us, so if we want to conserve the dolphins and their environment we must ask the relevant questions.

Bottlenose Dolphins Facts

Scientific name: *Tursiops truncatus*

FACT	SEX	Florida, USA	Britain/Europe
Adult Length:	Male	104 in (265 cm)	161.5 in (410 cm)
	Female	98.5 in (250 cm)	128 in (325 cm)
	Newborn Calf	46-55 in (116-140 cm)	(data from Japan)
Adult Weight:	Male	573 lb (260 kg)	(no data available)
	Female	419 lb (190 kg)	(no data available)
Age at sexual maturity:	Male	10-13 years	10-13 years
	Female	7-12 years	7-12 years
Gestation period		1 year	1 year
No of calves		1 usually born in summer	1 usually born in summer

Recommended Reading

Dolphins by Ben Wilson, Grantown-on-Spey, 1998

The Sierra Club Handbook of Whales and Dolphins by Stephen Leatherwood and Randall Reeves, San Francisco, 1983. A pocket-sized guide to the world's different cetacean species.

The Bottlenose Dolphin: Biology & Conservation, John E Reynolds III, Randall S Wells & Samantha D Eide, Miami, 2000.

The Bottlenose Dolphin, ed. by Stephen Leatherwood and Randall Reeves, London, 1989. A collection of scientific essays by some of the leading researchers on bottlenose dolphins.

Biographical Notes

Paul Thompson is a senior lecturer in the Department of Zoology at the University of Aberdeen. He is based at the Department's Lighthouse Field Station, where he co-ordinates a long-term research program on the ecology of seals and dolphin populations in the Moray Firth.

Ben Wilson is a research scientist at the Sea Mammal Research Unit, University of St Andrews. He carried out his Ph.D at the University of Aberdeen on the community of bottlenose dolphins in the Moray Firth. Since then he has continued studying and writing about dolphins in Europe and North America.

Index